NATIONAL
GEOGRAPHIC

# book of animal poetry

With favorites from Robert Frost, Jack Prelutsky, Emily Dickinson, and more

## 200 poems with photographs that SQUEAK, SOAR, and ROAR!

Edited by J. Patrick Lewis, U.S. Children's Poet Laureate

NATIONAL
GEOGRAPHIC

WASHINGTON, D.C.

# the strange ones      102-123

# the noisy ones      124-145

# ✳ the quiet ones      146-163

# Final Thought      164-169

J. PATRICK LEWIS HAS WRITTEN MORE THAN 75 PICTURE AND POETRY BOOKS FOR YOUNG READERS. IN 2011, HE WAS APPOINTED U.S. CHILDREN'S POET LAUREATE, AND WAS GIVEN THE NATIONAL COUNCIL OF TEACHERS OF ENGLISH EXCELLENCE IN CHILDREN'S POETRY AWARD.

RED FOX

# HAVE YOU ever thought about a day in the life of a giraffe, a porcupine, a whale, or a snail?

At this very moment, each one of them (if they are not asleep) is bustling about, fast or slow, as busy in his day, in her way, as you are in yours. Whether they live underground, on the ice, in the desert, the sea, the rain forest—or under your front porch—animals all over the world are searching for something very important: food or mates. Or maybe just the company of family and friends and the blue sky above. These creatures, like some of their human companions, seem to appreciate most of all the simple joys of exploring their worlds.

As you will see in this book, poets often try to imagine the secret lives of animals. For instance, what does any pig really need? Myra Cohn Livingston knows what makes a pig happy on a rainy day as well as in "Summertime." You may have guessed already, but Alice Schertle cleverly tells us why "The Bull" can't keep himself from always acting like such a big shot. John Agard lists angry names for an alligator, but warns us not to use any of them until we have crossed the river safely!

The poems in these pages resonate with wonder at the variety, beauty, and strangeness of the animal world around us. As you read them, you may think, *I never thought of a caterpillar, a starfish, or an elephant in that way before.* That's what all poets hope you will say after you have read their poems. And if the poet succeeds, then you may re-member a line or two—and the animal for whom the lines were written—long after you have finished reading the poem.

This book is not for reading straight through. Pick it up anytime. Choose a poem and then read it out loud: You want your ears to have as much fun as your mouth is having. Take the book to the doctor, the dentist, or put it in your book bag. Once you have opened it, you are likely to find words that are not so much a description as a revelation.

And the pictures are pretty nice, too!

*—J. Patrick Lewis, U.S. Children's Poet Laureate*

# WELC
## TO THE
# WORLD

AMERICAN ROBIN

OME

## The Egg

If you listen very carefully, you'll hear the chicken hatching.
At first there scarcely was a sound, but now a steady scratching;
and now the egg begins to crack, the scratching begins to quicken,
as anxiously we all await the exit of the chicken.

And now a head emerges from the darkness of the egg,
and now a bit of fluff appears, and now a tiny leg,
and now the chicken's out at last, he's shaking himself loose.
But, wait a minute, that's no chicken . . . goodness, it's a goose.

—*Jack Prelutsky*

## The Tickle Rhyme

"Who's that tickling my back?" said the wall.
"Me," said a small
Caterpillar.
"I'm learning
To crawl."

—Ian Serraillier

## What's a Caterpillar?

Little
but a fly
in waiting.

—Graham Denton

MONARCH
CATERPILLAR

# Cocoon

The little caterpillar creeps
Awhile before in silk it sleeps.
It sleeps awhile before it flies,
And flies a while before it dies,
And that's the end of three good tries.

—David McCord

MONARCH BUTTERFLY CHRYSALIS

BALI SARDINES

# Haiku

Dancing through the waves,
ballerinas of the blue—
the ocean their stage.

—*Joan Bransfield Graham*

# THE BIG
## ONES

# Buffalo Dusk

The buffaloes are gone.
And those who saw the buffaloes are gone.
Those who saw the buffaloes by the thousands and how they
    pawed the prairie sod into dust with their hoofs,
    their great heads down pawing on in a great pageant
    of dusk,
Those who saw the buffaloes are gone.
And the buffaloes are gone.

    —*Carl Sandburg*

# Wedding Bears

A panda by the name of Ling-
Ling met another panda, Ping.
They fell in love the first of spring
And hand in hand, Ling-Ling and Ping
Planned a panda wedding-ding.
A fling,
A ring,
A wedding-ding!
The sun was shining.
So was Ling-
Ling standing
Hand in hand with Ping.

—*J. Patrick Lewis*

GIANT PANDAS

# The Purple Cow

I never saw a Purple Cow,
   I never hope to see one,
But I can tell you anyhow,
   I'd rather see than be one.

*—Gelett Burgess*

# Cow

The cow
Coming
Across the grass
Moves
Like a mountain
Toward us;
Her hipbones
Jut
Like sharp
Peaks
Of stone,
Her hoofs
Thump
Like dropped
Rocks:
Almost
Too late
She stops.

*—Valerie Worth*

# A Farmer's Boy

They strolled down the lane together,
The sky was studded with stars—
They reached the gate in silence
And he lifted down the bars—
She neither smiled nor thanked him
Because she knew not how;
For he was just a farmer's boy
And she was a jersey cow.

—Anonymous

VALDOSTANA COWS

# The Cow

The friendly cow all red and white,
 I love with all my heart;
She gives me cream with all her might,
 To eat with apple tart.

She wanders lowing here and there,
 And yet she cannot stray,
All in the pleasant open air,
 The pleasant light of day;

And blown by all the winds that pass
 And wet with all the showers,
She walks among the meadow grass
 And eats the meadow flowers.

—Robert Louis Stevenson

# The Pasture

I'm going out to clean the pasture spring;
I'll only stop to rake the leaves away
(And wait to watch the water clear, I may):
I sha'n't be gone long.—You come too.

I'm going out to fetch the little calf
That's standing by the mother. It's so young
It totters when she licks it with her tongue.
I sha'n't be gone long.—You come too.

—Robert Frost

21

# Dear Orangutan,

Three cheers to you, man of the forest.
You arrived here long before us.
You paved the way; you saw it through.
Now nice to have someone like you
sitting in our family tree.

Sincerely, from your cousin,
Me

—David Elliott

ORANGUTANS

# mOOse

To introduce
the world of moose,
gather woodlands
stream and spruce.
Add antlers
scooping bits of sky;
pause to watch
in wonder—*sigh*,
as he dines on aspen, fir
carefully watching
out for her.

—*Rebecca Kai Dotlich*

# Song of a Bear

There is danger where I move my feet.
I am a whirlwind. There is danger where I move my feet.
I am a gray bear.
When I walk, where I step lightning flies from me.
Where I walk, one to be feared.
Where I walk, long life.
One to be feared I am.
There is danger where I walk.

*—A Navajo poem*

# Grandpa Bear's Lullaby

The night is long
But fur is deep.
You will be warm
In winter sleep.

The food is gone
But dreams are sweet
And they will be
Your winter meat.

The cave is dark
But dreams are bright
And they will serve
As winter light.

Sleep, my little cubs, sleep.

*—Jane Yolen*

# Elephant

The elephant carries a great big trunk;
He never packs it with clothes;
It has no lock and it has no key,
But he takes it wherever he goes.

—*Anonymous*

# Elephant

A threatening cloud, plumped fat and gray,
Snorts a thunder, rains a spray
And billows puffs of dust away—
A weather maker every day.

—*Ann Whitford Paul*

# Eletelephony

Once there was an elephant,
Who tried to use the telephant—
No! No! I mean an elephone
Who tried to use the telephone—
(Dear me! I am not certain quite
That even now I've got it right.)
Howe'er it was, he got his trunk
Entangled in the telephunk;
The more he tried to get it free,
The louder buzzed the telephee—
(I fear I'd better drop the song
Of elephop and telephong!)

—*Laura E. Richards*

# Anthology

So many stories
Locked inside the amber eye
Of one elephant

—*Tracie Vaughn Zimmer*

ASIAN ELEPHANT

# The Whales
# Off Wales

With walloping tails, the whales off Wales
Whack waves to wicked whitecaps.
And while they snore on their watery floor,
They wear wet woolen nightcaps.

The whales! the whales! the whales off Wales,
They're always spouting fountains.
And as they glide through the tilting tide,
They move like melting mountains.

—X. J. Kennedy

# Polar Bear Rap

Weather be chillin',
Weather be nice
Whether we swimmin'
Up under de ice.

Weather be sleetin',
Weather be snow
Whether we stayin'
But we gotta go.

Weather be nuttin'
'Less me 'n' you
Bust on outta this
Nuttin' much zoo.

—*J. Patrick Lewis*

# Polar Bear

Every time
I stand and stare
At the big
White polar bear,
I wonder
While he's
Swimming there,
If he has on
Long underwear.

—*Leland Blair Jacobs*

# Moody Guy

Boulders for shoulders,
Elegant horn—
A pointed reminder of the
Unicorn,
Thick leg-pillars bruising tawny
Yellow grass

In huge hide shoes,
Nobody argues

This is a colossal
Holdover from
Earth's primeval swamp.

But
Even so, I know
A rhino when I
See one, and this is the time not
To.

—Avis Harley

# The White Rhinoceros

I took a number 7 bus
To see the White Rhinoceros.

I rang the bell. He let me in
And said, "Hello. How have you been?"

I told him all my hopes and fears.
He looked at me and flicked his ears.

I told him all my fears and hopes.
He handed me two telescopes.

I questioned him about his horn.
He said, "Before the world was born."

"But how," I asked him, "can that be?"
He said, "And now it's time for tea."

I left his house at half-past-four.
He chuckled as he shut the door.

—Stephen Mitchell

# Tiger

There was a young lady of Niger
Who smiled as she rode on a tiger.
　They returned from the ride
　　With the lady inside—
And the smile on the face of the tiger.

—*Anonymous*

# Giraffe

How lucky
To live
So high
Above
The body,
Breathing
At heaven's
Level,
Looking
Sun
In the eye;
While down
Below
The neck's
Precarious
Stair,
Back, belly,
And legs
Take care
Of themselves,
Hardly
Aware
Of the head's
Airy
Affairs.

—Valerie Worth

# Above All

Celebrate these
Long-standing giraffes,
Opening
Up clouds and eaves-
Dropping on the wind!

Far
Removed
In airy
Elegance,
Nibbling on high, they
Decorate the
Sky.

—Avis Harley

# The Hippopotamus

I shoot the Hippopotamus
With bullets made of platinum.
Because if I used leaden ones
His hide is sure to flatten 'em.

—Hilaire Belloc

HIPPOPOTAMUS

# The Horses

It has turned to snow in the night.
The horses have put on
their long fur stockings
and they are wearing
fur caps with high necks
out of which the device
of their ears makes four statues.
Their tails have caught flecks
of snow and hang down
loose as bedsheets.
They stand nose to nose
in the blue light that coats
the field before sunup
and rub dry their old kisses.

*—Maxine Kumin*

# The Horseman

I heard a horseman
   Ride over the hill;
The moon shone clear,
   The night was still;
His helm was silver,
   And pale was he;
And the horse he rode
   Was of ivory.

*—Walter de la Mare*

# Horses

Back and forth
and up and down
horses' tails go switching.

Up and down
and back and forth
horses' skins go twitching.

Horses do
a lot of work
to keep themselves from itching.

—*Aileen Fisher*

## The **White Horse**

The youth walks up to the white horse, to put its halter on
and the horse looks at him in silence.
They are so silent, they are in another world.

—*D. H. Lawrence*

WESTERN LOWLAND GORILLA

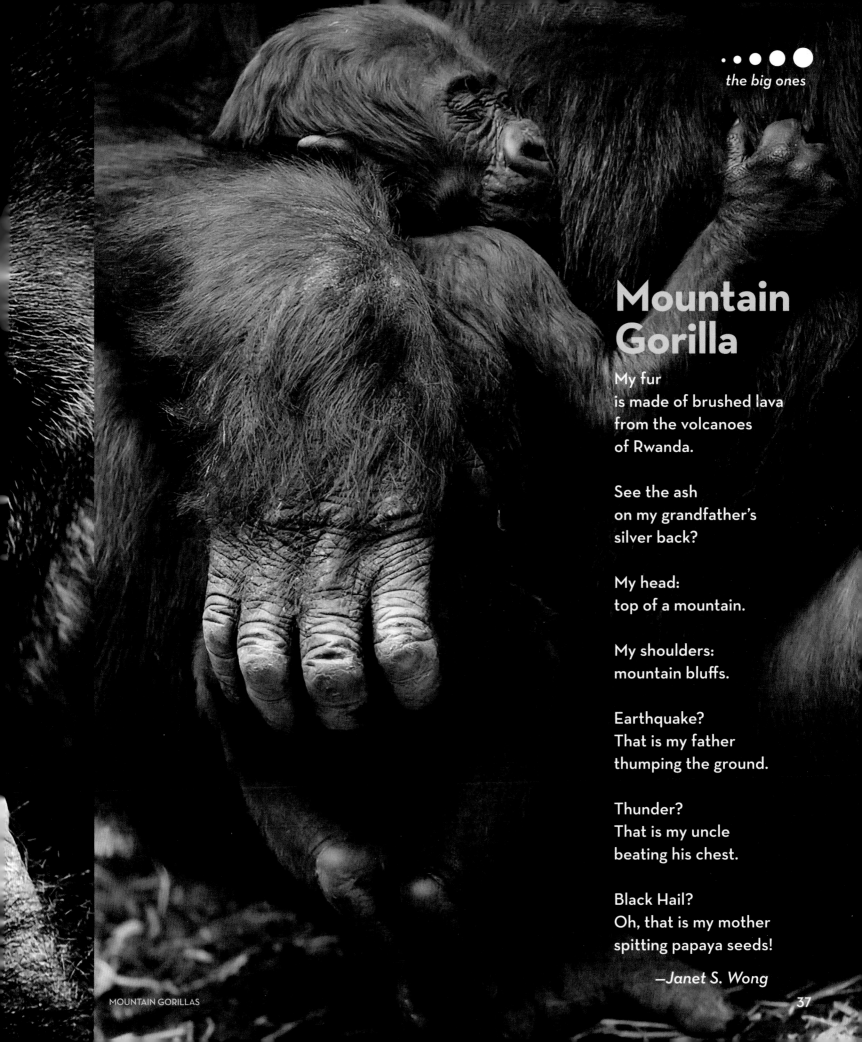

# Mountain Gorilla

My fur
is made of brushed lava
from the volcanoes
of Rwanda.

See the ash
on my grandfather's
silver back?

My head:
top of a mountain.

My shoulders:
mountain bluffs.

Earthquake?
That is my father
thumping the ground.

Thunder?
That is my uncle
beating his chest.

Black Hail?
Oh, that is my mother
spitting papaya seeds!

—Janet S. Wong

# THE LITTLE ONES

# Ladybug

Smaller
than a button,
bigger than a spot
this crimson queen
with midnight polished
polka dots
journeys in
her ruby shell,
across
the walks,
along
the cracks,
among
the petals of a rose—
carefully,
tenderly she goes.

—*Rebecca Kai Dotlich*

# Ants

One and one and one and one
    Dead leaves
    Dead crickets
One ant alone can't pick it
    up
can't drag this meal to our busy nest
But one and one and one and one
    Together we tow
    Together we know
any time of day this is so:
One and one and one and one
    is the best way
    to get things done

—Marilyn Singer

# Solitude

There now, where the first crumb
Falls from the table
You think no one hears it
As it hits the floor

But somewhere already
The ants are putting on
Their Quakers' hats
And setting out to visit you.

—Charles Simic

WEAVER ANT

# Dragonfly

It skims the pond's surface,
searching for gnats, mosquitoes, and flies.
Outspread wings blur with speed.
It touches down
and stops to sun itself on the dock.
Wings flicker and still:
stained-glass windows
with sun shining through.

*—Georgia Heard*

# Grasshoppers Three

Grasshoppers three a-fiddling went,
Hey-ho, never be still!
They paid no money toward their rent
But all day long with elbow bent
They fiddled a tune called "Rill-a-be, rill-a-be"
Fiddled a tune called "Rill-a-be-rill."

—An old song

GRASSHOPPERS

43

# Little Fish

The tiny fish enjoy themselves
in the sea.
Quick little splinters of life,
their little lives are fun to them
in the sea.

—*D. H. Lawrence*

BLUESTREAK
FUSILIER

GORGONIAN CORAL AND
FEATHER STAR

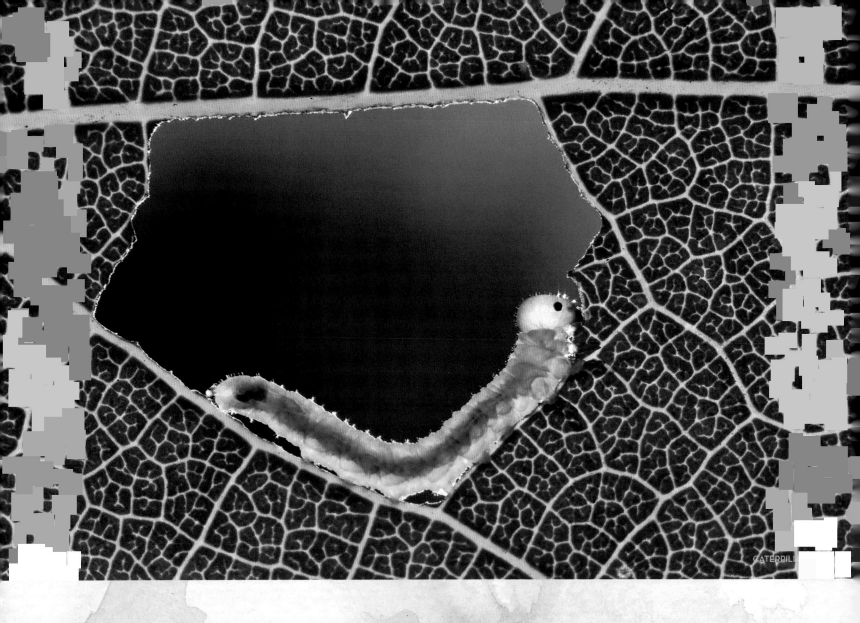

# The **Caterpillar**

The caterpillar's not a cat.
It's very small
And short and fat,
And with those beady little eyes
Will never win a beauty prize.
The caterpillar's brain is small—
It only knows to eat and crawl.
But for this creepy bug don't cry,
It soon will be a butterfly.

—Douglas Florian

# **Caterpillar**

Caterpillar. Bulgy. Brown.
Creeping up the rose.
Soon he will be beautiful
In his party clothes.

—Tony Johnston

# The **Butterfly**

A book of summer is the butterfly:
The print is small and hard to read,
The pages ruffle in the wind,
And when you close them up they die.

—John Fuller

# **Butterfly**

What is a butterfly?
At best
He's but a caterpillar
Dressed.

—Benjamin Franklin

TIGER SWALLOWTAIL
BUTTERFLY

# Cockroach sandwich

Cockroach sandwich
For my lunch
Hate the taste
But love the crunch!

—Colin McNaughton

# The Scorpion

The scorpion is as black as soot.
He dearly loves to bite;
He is a most unpleasant brute
To find in bed, at night.

—Hilaire Belloc

INCHWORM

# Inch**worm**

You have no reason for alarm
should an inchworm climb your arm.
Hunching, stretching, does no harm.

You're just an observation post
he'll cling on for a minute at most,
then make the switch to another host.

—*Michael J. Rosen*

# Inch by Inch

**Wiggle**
over here, dear—
**scribble** through mud puddles
**with me** by fractions and inches
of spring.

—*Rebecca Kai Dotlich*

# Rich Lizard

The rich lizard
shed his skin
of silver coins,
dropping them
in the dry grass.
Strange-wild thoughts
shook him,
warming his blood
to grander things,
and he tore himself
loose—
ran off,
leaving behind
his wealth of cold coins.

—*Deborah Chandra*

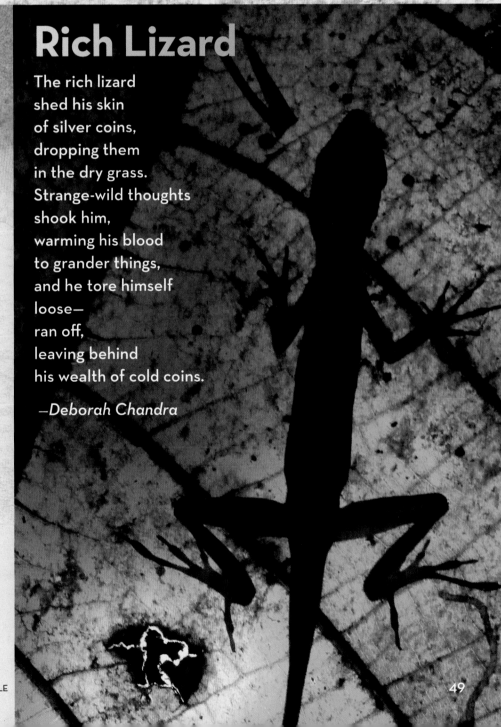

GREEN ANOLE

49

# The Chipmunk

My friends all know why I am shy,
But the chipmunk is twice as shy as I.
He moves with flickering indecision
Like stripes across the television.
He likes the shadow of a cloud,
Or Emily Dickinson read aloud.

—Ogden Nash

EASTERN CHIPMUNK

## Squirrel Forgets

Where
where
where
did I bury
that nut,

that sweet plump
nut that I carried
away?

Where
did I stop?
Where did I drop

that fat ripe nut
that I saved for
today?

Did I hide it
deep and far, or
near?

And why's a new green
nut tree growing
here?

—*Lilian Moore*

## Spruce Woods

It's so still
today that a
dipping bough means
a squirrel
has gone through.

—*A. R. Ammons*

WESTERN GRAY SQUIRREL

# Polliwogs

Come see
What I found!
Chubby commas,
Mouths round,
Plump babies,
Stubby as toes.
Polliwogs!
Tadpoles!

Come see
What I found!
Frogs-in-waiting—
Huddled in puddles,
Snuggled in mud.

—Kristine O'Connell George

GLASS FROGS

# Oh the Toe-Test!

The fly, the fly,
in the wink of an eye,
can taste with his feet
if the syrup is sweet
or the bacon is salty.
Oh is it his fault he
gets toast on his toes
as he tastes as he goes?

*—Norma Farber*

# The Spider Is a Lovely Lady

The spider is a lovely lady.
She knows just what to do.
She weaves a dainty web
to catch the morning dew.

The spider is a lovely lady.
She lives among the trees.
Her babies are so small
they float upon the breeze.

They spin a silken thread
that lifts them in the air.
"Take me home," they whisper.
And it brings them there.

—*Frank Asch*

CUCUMBER SPIDER

## I Am a Snail

I am a Snail
And my tell-trail
Is what I leave
Behind. Believe
Me when I say
I'm built this way—
My tummy slime
Is scummy. I'm
A crawling mess
Of stickiness,
And in my wake,
Make no mistake,
Is my distur-
bing signature.

—Anonymous

## Riddle

No matter where I travel.
No matter where I roam.
No matter where I find myself.
I always am at home.

Sniffed the snail
In its shell,
"This fact is true
Of me as well."

—Mary Ann
Hoberman

## from The Snail

To grass, or leaf, or fruit, or wall,
The Snail sticks close, nor fears to fall,
As if he grew there, house and all
Together.

—William Cowper

## Snail

The snail is skilled at going slow:
    It spans the earth by inches.
Where it has gone a trail will show.
    Its brave horn seldom flinches.

A dome of chalk upon its back,
    It lets a mayfly ride it
And when at night it goes to sleep
    It curls itself inside it.

—X. J. Kennedy

# Bee

You want to make some honey?
All right. Here's the recipe.
Pour the juice of a thousand flowers
Through the sweet tooth of a Bee.

—*X. J. Kennedy*

# Move Over

Big
burly
bumblebee
buzzing
through the grass,
move over.

Black and
yellow
clover rover,
let me pass.

Fat and
furry
rumblebee
loud on the
wing,
let me
hurry
past
your sting.

—*Lilian Moore*

# The Pedigree of Honey

The Pedigree of Honey
Does not concern the Bee—
A Clover, any time, to him,
Is Aristocracy—

—*Emily Dickinson*

# A Bee

A bee
staggers out
of the peony.

—*Matsuo Basho, translated
by Robert Hass*

## A Mouse of My Acquaintance

He thinks whatever's mine is his.
He lives with me but pays no rent,
And now I learn the mouse's Ms.,
To my utter astonishment,
Sleeps in my shoe.

The sneaky lodger and his wife,
Who may be sweet for all I know,
Have made a shambles of my life:
Two pickpockets on tippy-toe.
What can I do?

A mouse alone might be a friend;
Two mice are more than just one pair.
Two mice? That pair will never end.
The last time that I counted there
Were twenty-two!

—Anonymous

## The City Mouse and the Garden Mouse

The city mouse lives in a house;
    The garden mouse lives in a bower,
He's friendly with the frogs and toads,
    And sees the pretty plants in flower.

The city mouse eats bread and cheese;
    The garden mouse eats what he can;
We will not grudge him seeds and stalks,
    Poor little, timid, furry man.

—*Christina Georgina Rossetti*

# Hamster Hide-and-Seek

Over my arm
she softly flows—
cinnamon coat
and whiskery nose.

With marble eyes
she stops and peeks;
lets me stroke
her knapsack cheeks.

Then ripple-of-fur
takes her leave
to probe new roads
inside my sleeve.

—*Avis Harley*

RUSSIAN DWARF HAMSTER

# THE W I N G

E
D
ONES

# Three Little Owls Who Sang Hymns

There were three little owls in a wood
Who sang hymns whenever they could;
What the words were about
One could never make out,
But one felt it was doing them good.

—Anonymous

# A Wise Old Owl

A wise old owl lived in an oak
The more he saw the less he spoke
The less he spoke the more he heard.
Why can't we all be like that wise old bird?

—*A nursery rhyme*

# Haiku

*Listen . . . in the woods
a snowy owl is eating
the wind's syllable*

—*Anonymous*

# I Talk With the Moon

I talk with the moon, said the owl
While she lingers over my tree
I talk with the moon, said the owl
And the night belongs to me.

I talk with the sun, said the wren
As soon as he starts to shine
I talk with the sun, said the wren
And the day is mine.

—*Beverly McLoughland*

# Gray Goose

Gray mama goose
in a tizzy,
honk-honk-honking herself dizzy,
can't find her gosling,
she's honking and running,
webbed feet slapping,
all wild waddle,
her feathers a muddle,
splashing through puddles,
wings flapping. . . .

Ah,
there's her gold baby,
all fuzz,
napping.

—Julie Larrios

CANADA GEESE

# Moon Geese

You pressed the cold
circle against my eye,
I jumped back,
the moon so close
I thought it stuck
to the end of the telescope.

Then a dark fleck showed,
grew darker, longer,
and I shouted at
six geese rowing
across a full moon.

—Ann Turner

CANADA GEESE

# What Was That?

Ducks catapult into the water.
Herons' stilt legs trail
their sudden flight to
somewhere safer.

Flat shells smack the lake,
bony heads resurface,
stare at forsaken thrones.

What was that?

Maybe nothing.
A dog barked,
a child ran,
a turtle slipped.
All's clear
on the lip of the lake,
for now.

—David L. Harrison

# De Grey Goose

The preacher went a-huntin'
Lawd, Lawd, Lawd.
The preacher went a-huntin'
Lawd, Lawd, Lawd.
(Repeat pattern for each verse)

He carried 'long his shotgun.
'Long came a grey goose.
The gun went "a-boo-loo!"
Down came a grey goose.
He was six weeks a-fallin'.
Then they give a feather-pickin'.
Yo' wife an' my wife.
They was six weeks a-pickin'.
So they put him on to parboil.
He was six weeks a-boilin'.
So they put him on the table.
Fork couldn't stick him.
Knife couldn't cut him.
So they took him to the hog-pen,
Broke the sow's teeth out.

—Huddie Ledbetter

# Puzzling

Here's a fact that will cause you to frown—
Instead of growing up a goose grows down.

—William Cole

CANADA GOOSE

## Blue Jay

Blue Jay raises his
crest and shrieks out to the flock,
"Hawk incoming! Fight!"

—*Janet S. Wong*

# Dust of Snow

The way a crow
Shook down on me
The dust of snow
From a hemlock tree
Has given my heart
A change of mood
And saved some part
Of a day I had rued.

—*Robert Frost*

CROW

# The Blackbird

In the far corner
close by the swings,
every morning
a blackbird sings.

His bill's so yellow,
His coat's so black,
that he makes a fellow
whistle back.

Ann, my daughter,
thinks that he
sings for us two
especially.

—*Humbert Wolfe*

EURASIAN BLACKBIRD

67

# The **Eagle**

He clasps the crag with crooked hands
Close to the sun in lonely lands,
Ringed with the azure world, he stands.

The wrinkled sea beneath him crawls;
He watches from his mountain walls,
And like a thunderbolt he falls.

—*Alfred, Lord Tennyson*

BALD EAGLE

# Mother's Plea

Silence sirens.

Hush all horns.

Quiet rumbling

traffic roars.

Please
city

have
some
pity.

Promise me

not
one
more
beep?

My newborn

pigeons
need
their
sleep.

*—Lee Bennett Hopkins*

# Coastal Bats

Coastal bats
enjoy the view
from high on cliffs
in misty caves.
They like to watch
the frisky waves
when the sea is wild
and misbehaves.

—*Calef Brown*

VAMPIRE BAT

# A Warbler

In the sedge a tiny song
Wells and trills the whole day long;
In my heart another bird
Has its music heard.

As I watch and listen here,
Each to each pipes low and clear;
But when one has ceased to sing,
Mine will still be echoing.

—Walter de la Mare

# The Saddest Noise

The saddest noise, the sweetest noise,
    The maddest noise that grows,—
The birds, they make it in the spring,
    At night's delicious close.

—Emily Dickinson

# Birds in the Garden

Greedy little sparrow,
    Great big crow,
Saucy little chickadee,
    All in a row.

Are you very hungry,
    No place to go?
Come and eat my breadcrumbs,
    In the snow.

—Anonymous

# from Sing-Song

"Kookoorookoo! kookoorookoo!"
Crows the cock before the morn;
"Kikirikee! kikirikee!"
Roses in the east are born.

"Kookoorookoo! kookoorookoo!"
Early birds begin their singing;
"Kikirikee! kikirikee!"
The day, the day, the day is springing.

—Christina Georgina Rossetti

# Inuit Song

SEA GULL
who flaps his wings
over my head
                    in the blue air,

you GULL up there
dive down
              come here
take me with you
                    in the air!

Wings flash by
my mind's eye
and I'm up there sailing
in the cool air,
              a-a-a-a-a-ah,

                    in the air.

*—translated by Edward Field,*
*after Nakasuk*

# Haiku

Frantic sandpiper
high tides erasing
her footnotes

*—Anonymous*

BLACK-HEADED GULL

# Visitor

A spark, a glint,
  a glimpse
  of pixie tidbit.
Bright flits, brisk zips,
  a green-gray blur,
  wings, zings, and *whirr*—

I just heard
  a humming of bird.

—*Kristine O'Connell George*

# You Can Talk About Your Hummingbirds

on hot june afternoons          sticking
                                noses

into sweet clematis blooms
and
talk about goldfinch feathers
        against green leaves
but
during winter
        winter mornings
we are
    the gray birds of the yards

        sometimes in march
the only moving
        things on frozen
                        air

—*Arnold Adoff*

# Hummingbird

I'm The Nectar Inspector,
Sweetness Detector–
I sip–
I don't sniff.
I love juice
not perfume.
In its deep-throated scarlet
cup of a bud
(Beardtongue) Penstemon's
my favorite brew!

—*Janet S. Wong*

# Haiku

A bitter morning:
sparrows sitting together
without any necks.

*—J. W. Hackett*

WHITE-THROATED SPARROW

## Arrivals

The swallows light
on sloping wires,
then tails flicking
they slice the clouds
more delicate than surgeons,
let summer in.

—*Ann Turner*

# The **White** Egret

**The white egret**

**marks time**

**on**

**one**

**leg**

**then**

**the**

**other.**

*—Paul Janeczko*

# The **Parrot**

I am the pirate's parrot,
I sail the seven seas
And sleep inside the crow's nest
Don't look for me in trees!

I am the pirate's parrot,
A bird both brave and bold.
I guard the captain's treasure
And count his hoard of gold.

—*Anonymous*

BLUE AND YELLOW MACAW

# THE WATER ONES

# Penguins

Penguins waddle.
Penguins stroll
All around
The cold South Pole.

Penguins slide.
Penguins swim.
Penguins never
Look too slim.

Penguins play.
Penguins dress
Always in
Their Sunday best.

—*Charles Ghigna*

# The Penguin

The penguin sits upon the shore
And loves the little fish to bore.
He has one enervating joke
That would a very saint provoke:
"The *pen*-guin's mightier than the *sword*-fish."
He tells this daily to the bored fish
Until they are so weak they float
Without resistance down his throat.

—*Oliver Herford*

# Lost in the
# Cold

When a Penguin got lost at Peng. Station,
She was told at South Pole Information,
   "Next stop: Icy Pool,
   After that Supercool,
Then Eternal Refrigeration."

   —*Anonymous*

# Anemone

A flower with no smell,
A fisher with no line,
A trapper with no lure
Who, mouthless, still can dine.

A rider without legs,
A killer without hands
Who, silent, waits a lifetime
On shifting sea-soft sands.

—*Jane Yolen*

FISH-EATING ANEMONE

# The **Starfish**

When I see a starfish
Upon the shining sand,
I ask him how he liked the sea
And if he likes the land.
"Would you rather be a starfish
Or an out-beyond-the-bar fish?"
I whisper very softly,
And he seems to understand.

He never *says* directly,
But I fancy all the same
That he knows the answer quite as well
As if it were his name:
"An out-beyond-the-bar fish
Is much happier than a starfish";
And when I look for him again
He's gone the way he came.

—David McCord

# SEAL

See how he dives
   From the rocks with a zoom!
   See how he darts
      Through his watery room
      Past crabs and eels
      And green seaweed,
      Past fluffs of sandy
      Minnow feed!
      See how he swims
      With a swerve and a twist,
      A flip of the flipper,
      A flick of the wrist!
   Quicksilver-quick,
   Softer than spray,
Down he plunges
And sweeps away;
Before you can think,
Before you can utter
   Words like "Dill pickle"
   Or "Apple butter,"
      Back up he swims
      Past Sting Ray and Shark,
      Out with a zoom,
         A whoop, a bark;
         Before you can say
         Whatever you wish,
         He plops at your side
         With a mouthful of fish!

   —William Jay Smith

88

# The Performing Seal

Who is so proud
As not to feel
A secret awe
Before a seal
That keeps such sleek
And wet repose
While twirling candles
On his nose?

—*Rachel Field*

# Seal Lullaby

Oh! hush thee, my baby, the night is behind us,
And black are the waters that sparkled so green.
The moon, o'er the combers, looks downward to find us
At rest in the hollows that rustle between.
Where billow meets billow, there soft be thy pillow;
Ah, weary wee flipperling, curl at thy ease!
The storm shall not wake thee, nor sharks overtake thee,
Asleep in the arms of the slow-swinging seas.

—*Rudyard Kipling*

# The Walrus

The widdly, waddly walrus
has flippery, floppery feet.
He dives in the ocean for dinner
and stands on his noggin to eat.

The wrinkly, crinkly walrus
swims with a debonair splash.
His elegant tusks are of ivory
and he wears a fine walrus moustache.

The thundery, blundery walrus
has a rubbery, blubbery hide.
He puffs up his neck when it's bedtime
and floats fast asleep on the tide.

—Jack Prelutsky

# The Eel

I don't mind eels
Except as meals
And the way they feels.

—Ogden Nash

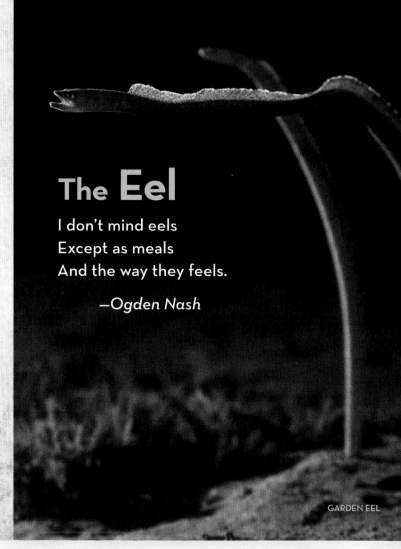

GARDEN EEL

WALRUS

# Beavers in November

This stick    here
That stick    there
   Mud, more mud, add mud, good mud
That stick    here
This stick    there
   Mud, more mud, add mud, good mud
     You pat
     I gnaw
     I pile
     You store
This stick    here
That stick    there
   Mud, more mud, add mud, good mud

     You guard
     I pack
     I dig
     You stack
That stick    here
This stick    there
   Mud, more mud, add mud, good mud
     I trim
     You mold
     To keep
     Out cold
This stick    here
That stick    there
   Mud, more mud, add mud, good mud

—*Marilyn Singer*

# There Was an
# Old Person of Hyde

**There was an old person of Hyde,**
**Who walked by the shore with his bride,**
**Till a Crab who came near, fill'd their bosoms with fear,**
**And they said, "Would we'd never left Hyde!"**

*—Edward Lear*

## Young Prince Pinch

Young Prince Pinch
was a jolly young prince
and a jolly young prince was he.
He sharpened his claws
and he sharpened his jaws
and he sharpened his pincers on me!

—*Avis Harley*

## The Crab

Don't ever grab
old crusty crab
because
with all those claws
he'll maybe grab you first
and you'll come off the worst!
I knew a small boy long ago
o long and long and long ago
whose mother said she did not know
just where the crab's eyes were: and so
he pointed with his finger, and
that crab politely took his hand
as if to say let's take a walk
and have a talk
upon this lovely seaside wharf:
and had to be flung off:
but on his finger left a dent
that lasted days before it went.
He doesn't sing he isn't mean
in fact he keeps the water clean
by eating up the scraps galore
that litter up the ocean's floor:
and if at times he can be vicious
remember he is so nutritious
and O in soups delicious!
(Perhaps it's mean
to mention a tureen.)
Old crusty crab, all claws no head,
he scuttles on the ocean bed
but never said
or so I've heard
a single crusty
or crustacean
word.

—*Conrad Aiken*

# Happy the Ocean

Angry the ocean
In hurricane season

Peaceful the ocean
Its whitecaps napping

Gloomy the ocean
As sky mirrors darken

Sunny the ocean
Yacht riggings snapping

Blue-green the ocean
In deep-shallow waters

Moody the ocean
Gone mad in a minute

Busy the ocean
With cargo and cruises

Happy the ocean
With dolphins in it

*—Anonymous*

# Sea Turtle

Inquisitive, she surveys the blue-black wilderness.
Alone, she seeks peace in the waving sargassum.
Noble, she spurns the long nets and the soup pots
    of greedy nations.
Driven, she navigates her island night landing
    to returtle the sea.
Fulfilled, she does not wait for the brash hatchling
    dash to the wall of gulls.
At eighty, she has seen enough of the wide wet world
    and is content with letting go.

—*Anonymous*

GREEN SEA TURTLE

# Turtles

Turtles sit.
Turtles wait.
Turtles never
Think they're late.

Turtles crawl.
Turtles snap.
Turtles take
A long, long nap.

Turtles listen.
Turtles hide.
Turtles like
To stay inside.

—*Charles Ghigna*

# The Shark

A treacherous monster is the Shark
He never makes the least remark.
And when he sees you on the sand,
He doesn't seem to want to land.
He watches you take off your clothes,
And not the least excitement shows.
His eyes do not grow bright or roll,
He has astonishing self-control.
He waits till you are quite undressed,
And seems to take no interest.
And when towards the sea you leap,
He looks as if he were asleep.
But when you once get in his range,
His whole demeanor seems to change.
He throws his body right about,
And his true character comes out.
It's no use crying or appealing,
He seems to lose all decent feeling.
After this warning you will wish
To keep clear of this treacherous fish.
His back is black, his stomach white,
He has a very dangerous bite.

—Lord Alfred Douglas

# About the
# Teeth of
# Sharks

The thing about shark teeth is—teeth,
One row above, one row beneath.

Now take a close look. Do you find
It has another row behind?

Still closer—here, I'll hold your hat:
Has it a third row behind that?

Now look in and . . . Look out! Oh my,
I'll *never* know now! Well, goodbye.

—*John Ciardi*

CARIBBEAN REEF SHARK

# Sea Jelly

It's not made of jelly; it isn't a fish.
Mostly it drifts, but can move with a swish.
It doesn't have lungs or a brain; most can't see.
It captures its dinner tentacularly.
Named after a Gorgon who turned men to stone,
It's best if you leave this Medusa alone.

—*Kelly Ramsdell Fineman*

BARREL JELLYFISH

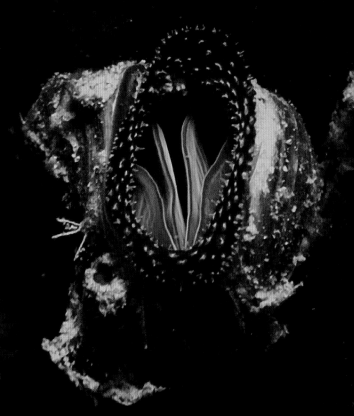

# Do Oysters Sneeze?

Do oysters sneeze beneath the seas,
or wiggle to and fro,
or sulk, or smile, or dance awhile
. . . how can we ever know?

Do oysters yawn when roused at dawn,
and do they ever weep,
and can we tell, when in its shell,
an oyster is asleep?

—*Jack Prelutsky*

# Mussel

One valve, two valve,
Mollusk, mussel,
Shells itself from
Hustle, bustle.
Keeping still is
No impediment.
Buried under
Muddy sediment.

But when it tires
Of life's low lull,
It hitches to
A tanker's hull
And rides the trade routes
While it can
From Kowloon Bay
North to Japan.

—*Steven Withrow*

ZEBRA MUSSEL

# Don't Call Alligator Long-Mouth Till You Cross River

Call alligator long-mouth
call alligator saw-mouth
call alligator pushy-mouth
call alligator scissors-mouth
call alligator raggedy-mouth
call alligator bumpy-bum
call alligator all dem rude word
　　　　　but better wait
　　　　　till you cross river.

　　　　　　　—John Agard

# The Crocodile

How doth the little crocodile
    Improve his shining tail,
And pour the waters of the Nile
    On every golden scale!

How cheerfully he seems to grin,
    How neatly spreads his claws,
And welcomes little fishes in,
    With gently smiling jaws!

            —Lewis Carroll

# Dark Meat

Once I had a crocodile
    For a pet.
Unfortunately, no one's
    Found me yet.

           —Anonymous

CROCODILE

# THE STRANGE ONES

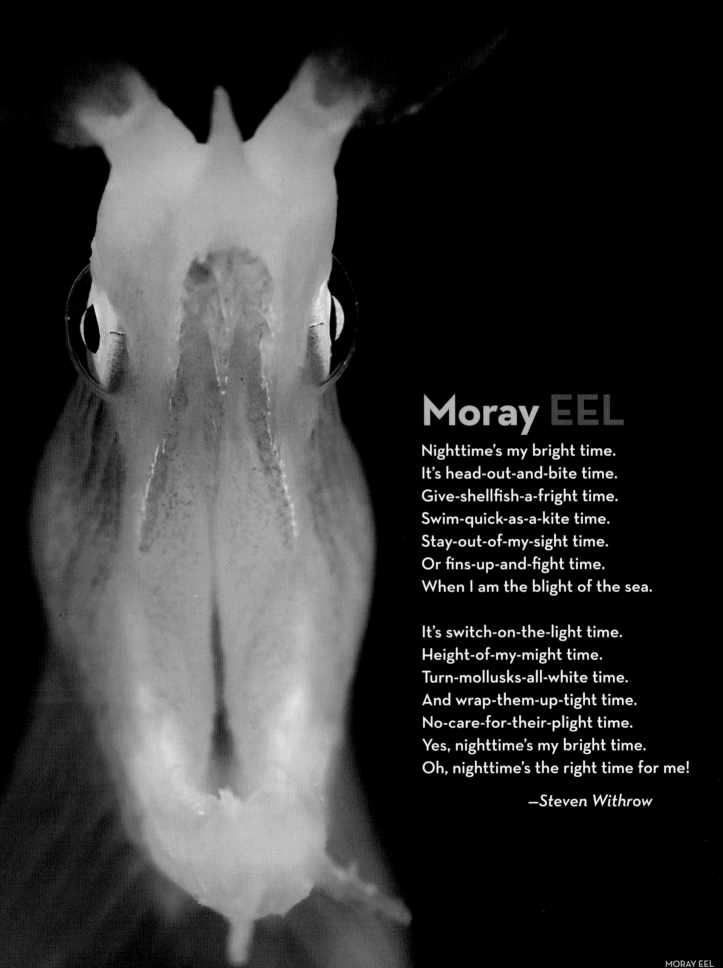

# Moray EEL

Nighttime's my bright time.
It's head-out-and-bite time.
Give-shellfish-a-fright time.
Swim-quick-as-a-kite time.
Stay-out-of-my-sight time.
Or fins-up-and-fight time.
When I am the blight of the sea.

It's switch-on-the-light time.
Height-of-my-might time.
Turn-mollusks-all-white time.
And wrap-them-up-tight time.
No-care-for-their-plight time.
Yes, nighttime's my bright time.
Oh, nighttime's the right time for me!

—*Steven Withrow*

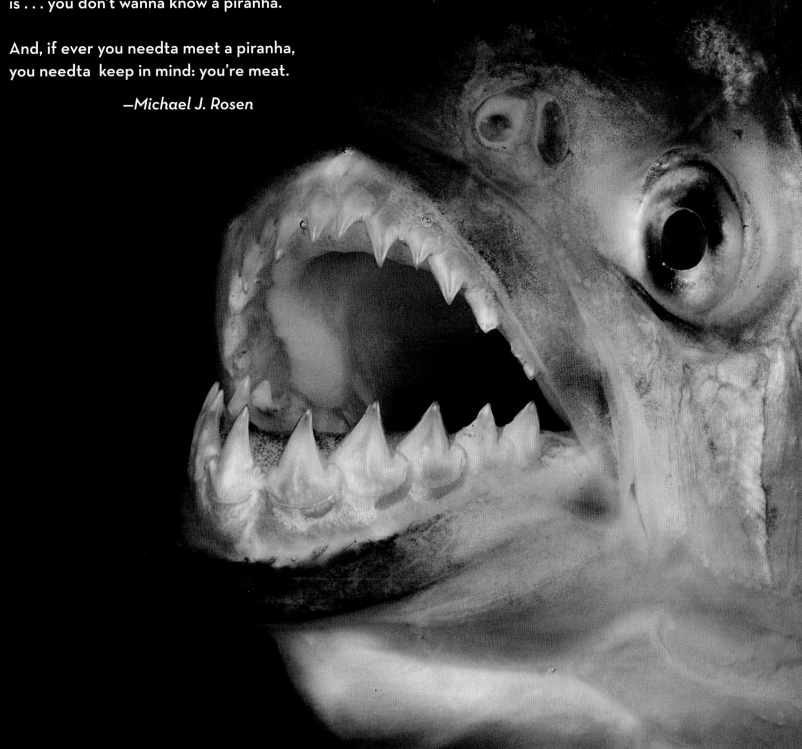

# All You **Oughta** Know About a Piranha

**All you wanna know about a piranha
is . . . you don't wanna know a piranha.**

**And, if ever you needta meet a piranha,
you needta  keep in mind: you're meat.**

*—Michael J. Rosen*

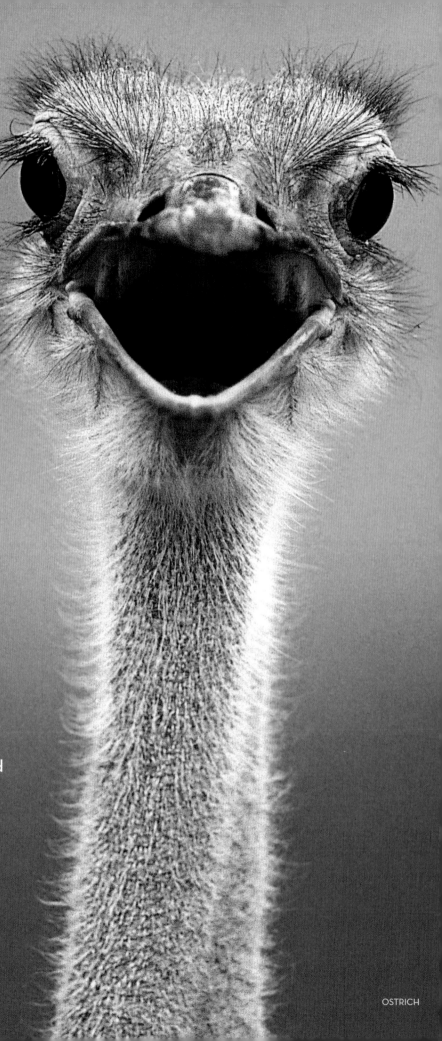

# The Ostrich

The ostrich roams the great Sahara.
Its mouth is wide, its neck is narra.
It has such long and lofty legs,
I'm glad it sits to lay its eggs.

—*Ogden Nash*

# The Ostrich Is a Silly Bird

The ostrich is a silly bird,
  With scarcely any mind.
He often runs so very fast,
  He leaves himself behind,

And when he gets there, has to stand
  And hang about till night,
Without a blessed thing to do
  Until he comes in sight.

—*Mary E. Wilkins Freeman*

# I Am a Baby Porcupette

I am a baby porcupette.
My paws are small; my nose is wet.
And as I nurse against my mom,
we mew and coo a soft duet.

I am a baby porcupette.
I cannot climb up branches yet.
While Mom sleeps in the trees, I curl
beneath a log till sun has set.

I am a baby porcupette.
I nibble in the nighttime wet:
a sprig of leaves, a tuft of grass,
in hidden spots I won't forget.

I am a baby porcupette.
My fur is soft; my eyes are jet.
But I can deal with any threat:
I raise my quills
                    and pirouette.

—Joyce Sidman

# Porcupine

Bedazzled by bristles,
bewhiskered with points,
lumbering
on clumsy joints—
shuffling along
knobby branch of pine;
rattling quills
    along his spine,
he nestles into
branch of chair,
settles down
to evening air—
tightly tucked
and in between
shade of spruce;
sweet evergreen,

quiet prince of timber, he
needles into limb
and tree;
claims this place—
ah, forest throne,
to wind and woodlands
    he calls home.

—Rebecca Kai Dotlich

# The **Octopus**

Tell me, O Octopus, I begs
Is those things arms,
or is they legs?
I marvel at thee,
Octopus;
If I were thou, I'd call me Us.

—*Ogden Nash*

# Seahorse

O under the ocean waves
I gallop the seaweed lanes,
I jump the coral reef,
And all with no saddle or reins.

I haven't a flowing mane,
I've only this horsy face,
But under the ocean waves
I'm king of the steeplechase.

—*Blake Morrison*

WEEDY SEA DRAGON

# What Is the
# Opposite of
# Pillow?

What is the opposite of *pillow*?
The answer, child, is *armadillo*.
"Oh, don't talk nonsense!" you protest.
However, if you tried to rest
Your head upon the creature, you
Would find that what I say is true.
It isn't soft. From head to tail
It wears a scratchy coat of mail.

And furthermore, it won't hold still
Upon a bed, as pillows will,
But squirms, and jumps at every chance
To run away and eat some ants.

So there! Admit that I was right,
Or else we'll have a *pillow fight*.

—*Richard Wilbur*

NINE-BANDED ARMADILLO

# The Anteater

The
    anteater's
        long
           and
              tacky
                  tongue
                      is
                     snaking
                          from
                            its
                            snout.

A thousand termites riding in,
But no one riding out.

         *—Douglas Florian*

# The Argument

The aardvark and the armadillo
can't decide which tastes the best.
"An anthill!" says the armadillo.
Aardvark insists, "A termite nest!"

    *—Bobbi Katz*

# Travel Plans

If I could go anywhere,
    here's what I'd do.
I'd pop in the pouch of a kind
    kangaroo.
I'd travel around for as long
    as I pleased,
And learn to say "thank you"
    in Kangarooese.

—*Bobbi Katz*

112

RED KANGAROO

# The Meerkats of Africa

Meerkats go about in packs,
They don't hang loose—
They're not really *cats* at all,
But more a mongoose.
They have great capabilities,
Make no mistake,
A Meerkat can kill a scorpion
Or even a snake.
They rescue each other's children
And have lookouts when they're feeding
And a system of babysitters—
The kind of co-operation
That the human race is needing!

—Gavin Ewart

# Sand Ghost

stingray resting
in the ocean sand
you're camouflaged
brown on tan,
then like a ghost
you rise and hover,
like a billow of brown
rippling around,
your arms spread wide
you glide and flap
then hide again
and disappear
were you ever here?

—*Betsy Franco*

ATLANTIC STINGRAY

# Frilled Lizard

*Expansion Collar*
*Instructions for Operation*

When not in use, the collar hangs
in compact folds of skin
conveniently tucked away
beneath the wearer's chin.

Activate the collar by
inflation of the lungs,
full extension of the jaws,
projection of the tongue.

Discourages a predator
two times out of three.
Batteries are not required.

Lifetime guarantee.

*—Alice Schertle*

# The Yak

As a friend to the children
  commend me the Yak.
   You will find it exactly the thing:
It will carry and fetch,
  you can ride on its back,
Or lead it about
  with a string.
The Tartar who dwells on the plains of Thibet
  (A desolate region of snow)
Has for centuries made it a nursery pet,
  And surely the Tartar should know!
Then tell your papa where the Yak can be got,
  And if he is awfully rich
He will buy you the creature—
  or else
        he will *not*.
(I cannot be positive which.)

—*Hilaire Belloc*

YAK

# How to **Tell** a **Camel**

The **D**romedary has one hump,
The **B**actrian has two.

It's easy to forget this rule,
So here is what to do.
Roll the first initial over
On its flat behind:

The **B**actrian is different from
The **D**romedary kind.

—*J. Patrick Lewis*

BACTRIAN CAMEL

# Skunk

Skunk
doesn't slink
but walks the earth
with a sense of worth

and wears with
pride
the bright white
stripe
on his inky
fur.

Skunk won't shrink,
to face a
foe.
Gives fair warning
"Better go!"
and many a foe
has slunk
away.

Skunk is
spunky,
mild as well,
and what a tale his
tail
could tell!

—*Lilian Moore*

MOLINA'S
HOG-NOSED
SKUNK

# A Flamingo Is

A Flamingo
is
a
long
coooooooooooooooool
drink
of
something
pink

—J. Patrick Lewis

# A
# Blue-footed
# Booby

You'd never see a bird who'd be
as shod as oddly as the booby.
It struts about on such blue legs
or poses on its clutch of eggs,
sharing baby brooding duties
until they hatch as newbie boobies.

**—Michael J. Rosen**

BLUE-FOOTED BOOBY

# Spoonbill
# Haiku

The princess of birds.
Her only competition
Is her reflection.

**—Jane Yolen**

ROSEATE SPOONBILL

119

# How to Paint a Zebra

To paint a zebra, mix the Moon
And Midnight in a can.
Roll it over and under
Shoulder to flank,
Belly to shank—
Midnight & Moon . . .

To zebriate the afternoon.

       *—Anonymous*

# Zebra

White men in Africa,
Puffing at their pipes,
Think the zebra's a white horse
With black stripes.

Black men in Africa,
With pipes of different types,
Know the zebra's a black horse
With white stripes.

       *—Gavin Ewart*

# Zebra

white sun
black
fire escape,

morning
grazing like a zebra
outside my window.

—*Judith Thurman*

# A Promise

Zebra, zebra—
wild and free
once you traveled
the African plains.
Caught and caged,
your freedom's gone,
but your wild beauty remains

Zebra, zebra—
one day soon
we'll gallop away
to the sea.
I won't keep you
in a cage.
Together, we both will be
free!

—*Bobbi Katz*

BURCHELL'S ZEBRAS

# A Centipede Was Happy Quite

A centipede was happy quite,
  Until a frog in fun
Said, "Pray, which leg comes after
    which?"
This raised her mind to such a pitch,
She lay distracted in the ditch
  Considering how to run.

—Anonymous

# Vanishing Act

Wait.
Is that a wayward dust bunny?
No.
it's the centipede—
a ballet of legs
gliding
skating
skimming
across the stage of white porcelain tile—
vanishing
behind the curtain of stage fright
before I've ever grabbed
a broom.

—Tracie Vaughn Zimmer

# Proboscis Monkey Ponders Man

The creature does nothing
but stand and stare.
Nobody knows
what he's doing there,
prowling the Primate Habitat,
finding someone
to ogle at.
Nobody knows
what he hopes to see,
gawking, squawking,
staring at me . . .
   Ha!
   Ha!
   Ha!
Tedious call.
His brain,
like his nose,
is probably
small.

—Alice Schertle

PROBOSCIS MONKEY

123

# THE NOISY ONES

CRAB-EATING MACAQUE

# The **Frog**

Be kind and tender to the Frog,
    And do not call him names,
As "Slimy-Skin," or "Polly-wog,"
    Or likewise,  "Ugly James,"
Or  "Gape-a-grin," or "Toad-gone-
        wrong,"
    Or "Billy-Bandy-knees";
The Frog is justly sensitive
    To epithets like these.

No animal will more repay
    A treatment kind and fair,
At least, so lonely people say
Who keep a frog (and, by the way,
    They are extremely rare).

                            —*Hilaire Belloc*

# The **BULL**

Do they watch me trot to the top of the hill,
the cows who are milling and mooing?
    I bellow and blow and paw the ground
    and make a sort of a snorting sound
    and toss my terrible horns around—
(*The cows—have they stopped their chewing?*)

I'm striking a pose; I'm standing still
as a statue here on the top of the hill.
    I flick my tail, as I stately stand,
    at a fool of a fly who has dared to land
    on the royal rump of a bull so grand—
(*Are they watching whatever I'm doing?*)

—*Alice Schertle*

# Bull and Ox

A *bull* acts like a bully
with a running start.
The ox enjoys a pull. He
tows any plow or cart.
One of them is slow and dull,
both of them are large.
One is unpredictabull—
he's the one in . . .

                c h a r g e!

—*Anonymous*

# Crickets

they    tell
the     time
of      night
they    tick

the     time
of      night
they    tick
they    tell

of      night
they    tick
and     tell
the     time

they    tick
they    tell
the     time
they    click

—*Myra Cohn Livingston*

# Splinter

The voice of the last cricket
across the first frost
is one kind of good-bye.
It is so thin a splinter of singing.

*—Carl Sandburg*

## Crickets

We cannot say that crickets sing
Since all they do is twang a wing.

Especially when the wind is still
They orchestrate a sunlit hill.

And in the evening blue above
They weave the stars and moon with love.

Then peacefully they chirp all night
Remembering delight, delight . . .

*—Harry Behn*

## Why Pigs Cannot Write Poems

Pigs cannot write poems because
Nothing rhymes with *oink*. If you
Think you can find a rhyme, I'll pause,
But if I wait until you do,
I'll have forgotten why it was
Pigs cannot write poems because.

*—John Ciardi*

## Pig

Pig, pig,
What have you brought me?

—Mud and a grunt and an oink.

Pig, pig,
What can I do
With mud and a grunt and an oink?

—With mud, said the pig,
You can wallow and play,
With a grunt, said the pig,
You can snooze all day,
With an oink, said the pig . . .
Then it dozed away.

So what can I do with this oink, I say,
What can I do with this oink?

*—Richard Edwards*

# Summertime

Was ever a pig
contented as this,
to roll in the mud
and know the bliss
of cooling off
in the muck
and grime,
having the grubbiest
mussiest
time?

and then, when he's cool,
to slowly rise
and dry himself off
in the summer skies,
and sniff for his supper
and slop up his feed—
What else
does a happy
piggy
need?

—*Myra Cohn Livingston*

# Piety

The pig is taught by sermons and epistles
To think the God of Swine has snout and bristles.

—*Ambrose Bierce*

# Dog

The sky is the belly of a large dog,
sleeping.
All day the small gray flag of his ear
is lowered and raised.
The dream he dreams has no beginning.

Here on earth we dream
a deep-eyed dog sleeps under our stairs
and will rise to meet us.
Dogs curl in dark places,
nests of rich leaves.
We want to bury ourselves
in someone else's home.

The dog who floats over us
has no master.
If there were people who loved him,
he remembers them equally,
the one who smelled like smoke,
the one who brought bones from the restaurant.
It is the long fence
of their hoping he would stay
that he has jumped.

—Naomi Shihab Nye

# Unpopular Rex

When our hound dog Rex
   Picked a fight with a skunk
It took ten weeks
   Till his atmosphere shrunk.

All that terrible while,
   Drooping tail, he fretted—
Why do they yell, he wondered,
   When I want to be petted?

—X. J. Kennedy

# The Breed
# You Need

If the dog you want has a pedigree,
Then the dog you want simply won't be me.
My crisscrossed bloodlines could derail a train
So the kennel club treats me with disdain.
Are you someone who loves a mystery?
Consider the clues; unlatch my history!
I've the best of this and the best of that
And "pedigree" soon will be so old hat.

If you want a dog with a heart that's true,
Then I am the dog who is meant for you.
The breed you need is spelled M-U-T-T.
I'm a marvelous mutt, so please choose me.

—*Bobbi Katz*